Footprints

Footprints

Peter Blackman

Published 2013 by
Smokestack Books
PO Box 408, Middlesbrough TS5 6WA
e-mail: info@smokestack-books.co.uk
www.smokestack-books.co.uk

Footprints
Peter Blackman

Typeset by EPW Print & Design Ltd, Hartlepool.
Printed and bound in the U.K. by Biddles, part of the
MPG Books Group Ltd, Bodmin & King's Lynn.

ISBN 978-0-9571722-8-9

Middlesbrough
moving forward

Smokestack Books is
represented by Inpress Ltd
www.inpressbooks.co.uk

Acknowledgements

I would like to thank the late Peter Blackman Jr. for talking to me about his father, Diana Binstead, Joe Martin, Buzz Johnson, Jenny Bourne, Hazel Waters, Ruth Tait and Andy Croft of Smokestack Books.
C.S.

Contents

Preface

Peter Blackman's poems were never published as a collection during his long lifetime (1909-1993), neither have they found a published edition in the two decades since his death, before *Footprints*. Yet I believe him to be a major Caribbean poet who embraced the real world around him – of black and exile politics, antifascist war and struggle, racial justice and the quest for a socialist society – unlike any other Caribbean or English poet of his generation. Throughout his life he defied and rejected fame, exposure and cultural fad or elitism. Perhaps this is why his remarkable poems have remained hidden from modern eyes. He was never part of an intelligentsia, fashionable or otherwise, or a populist poet. Neither was he a poet who was intellectually or politically introverted, or trapped within the individualised consciousness – a condition that has often been the predicament of the postmodern poet. His canvas was the world, its times and its politics; his subject and his readership, 'ordinary' people.

There is an assumption that British Caribbean poetry is almost entirely a post-Windrush phenomenon. Yet Blackman's poetry emerged from his London-exile during and just after the second world war, with a sense of optimism, hope and internationalism following the defeat of Nazism. All this gleaned by a powerfully (colonially) educated black man nonetheless working manually in a wartime aircraft factory building Wellington bombers and, postwar, as an engineer in a London railway repair depot. Not the traditional venues of eminent poets.

The post-1945 migrations of West Indian people to Britain (prefigured a generation and a half earlier by Blackman) transported a generation of arrivant writers like George Lamming and Edward Kamau Brathwaite (Barbadians); Sam Selvon (Trinidadian); Andrew Salkey and John Hearne (Jamaicans); and Jan Carew and Roy Heath (Guyanese). In this, they provoked major literary works focused either on life and conditions in their Caribbean homelands or on the experiences of West Indian communities in Britain. Other writers, like the Guyanese poet Martin Carter stayed in their home nations, hitching their words to domestic anti-colonial struggles.

Blackman was an exception. As a black communist in London, he drew his patterns of reference much more widely, defying race, geography and national origins. He wrote defiantly about racism and the struggle against it in sections of his 1948 poem, 'London'. But rather than restrict his focus to the colonial racism in his country of birth and boyhood, he wrote about it too in the American South, as in his poem 'Joseph' – a land where he had never lived but where, imaginatively, he was at one with American blacks' pursuit of their own struggle, faraway, for racial justice. From the centre of empire, he wrote out of an exiled Caribbean consciousness, as part of an international communist movement, as a low-paid industrial worker.

In these senses, he was an outsider, neither integral to the mass migration northwards of the postwar years or part of an anti-colonial process in his country of birth. His situation was that of a Caribbean revolutionary who was only partially accepted as a member of the mainly white, London Left. The black British communist Trevor Carter wrote in *Shattering Illusions* about the wastage by the British Left of his own postwar generation of West Indian migrants whose enormous 'talent and commitment … could and should have been [found] amongst the highest level of leadership in the labour and trade union movement [but] … which thwarted them and created a cynicism and despair that cannot fail to have been passed … to the next generation'.[1] Yet these comments applied even more to the far smaller generation of West Indians who had arrived and settled in pre-war England, of whom Blackman was one. (White 'comrades', as Carter declared, told their strongly committed Caribbean counterparts, some of them active communists, that they were merely 'on the periphery of development' and 'needed more time and expertise in the movement' before they could ever rise to any kind of leadership role.)

In the same way that Blackman's political capacities were left unutilised by the Left, so his poetic capacities developed at variance with the trends prevailing among his postwar contemporaries. He had passed through/been steeped in the extremely effective imperial enterprises of the exclusive colonial elite school and the church. He became a master of the language of both; his command of and ability to speak and write Standard English was effectively heightened by his years as a theology student at the prestigious, collegiate Durham University in the north of England. But in the post-Windrush years, when his worth as a poet should have been recognised and celebrated, Caribbean writing took a divergent path from the language that was Blackman's medium. Ironically, the languages of the 'ordinary' working people of the Caribbean, the Creole vernaculars – different in each island – took strength through, for example, the Trinidadian and London Caribbean novels of Selvon and the poetry of Louise Bennett and later Michael Smith of Jamaica, finding their apogee in the achievement of Blackman's Barbadian compatriot, Edward Kamau Brathwaite. Blackman's accomplished use of Standard English was deemed outmoded and even reactionary by the next generation of Caribbean writers. For they were earnest to discover and express themselves in the authenticity and beauty of their 'nation language', described, exemplified and discussed with brilliance in Brathwaite's epochal essay *History of the Voice*.[2] This was a poetry which, when allied with music, as with the rampant, figurative and rhythmically political words of Jamaican Londoner Linton Kwesi Johnson, defied categories, spoke to millions and glorified the truly popular tongue. But all this was a long way from Blackman's English.

And, finally, there was the man and the poet's own modest and retiring personal and literary demeanour. Despite his personal affability and friendliness, and even in the context of his remarkable life experiences and intelligence (he possessed what C. L. R. James referred to as 'great West Indian brains'), he was a deeply self-effacing and diffident man. 'I know I am very ordinary', he said of himself as an afterword to his comments on 'ordinariness' in an address given for Art Against Racism and Fascism, 'within a few years I shall be even less than ordinary. I am not interested in who reads my poems or who has ever heard of me. I am for the main part concerned really with trying to be alone.'[3] He rarely agreed to speak at meetings or read his poetry publicly, yet when he was asked to speak about the struggle against racism or fascism which had been at the centre of his cultural and political life, he agreed readily, needing no persuasion, expressing his ideas with fire, compassion and lucidity. And, like a golden thread through it all, ran his moving mastery of the English language, inflected as it was by the King James Bible, Milton, Blake and Whitman – all of which had been his life's inspiration.

So what do we know in more detail of Peter Blackman's life and work? One searcher's comment, who had been impressed by hearing a recording of Blackman's poem *Stalingrad*, is typical 'I have done a bit of internet searching but find very little about Blackman, who from what I can gather may have been of Afro-Caribbean origins. Oddly there are one or two other writers who refer to him in their own poetry, but very little about

Blackman himself.' What follows, I hope, will introduce
Blackman's life and work to a much wider audience,

From priesthood to politics

Peter Blackman was born in 1909 in St. John's Parish, one
of the poorer parts of Barbados. His father (who died when
he was two) was a stonemason and his mother a laundress.
He had three sisters, much older than him, who were
illiterate, and the family lived on Anglican Church grounds.
Perhaps this was why Peter's intelligence and potential were
noted by one of the local priests, who tutored him and
prepared him for entry to Harrison College, one the island's
elite schools. Here he was granted a scholarship through
the church, which saw him as a future 'native' recruit for
the priesthood. As he was later to write in his essay 'Is
there a West Indian Literature?' 'The Church knowing that
the Negro was not always quiescent, and true to the old
policy that one cassock is worth a regiment of soldiers,
worked hard to claim the Negro for religion.'⁴ Initially, he
was 'claimed'.

In order to succeed Blackman became soon persuaded that
within a British Caribbean colony 'England was the norm,
to be stamped 'Made in England' was the hallmark of
excellence'. This even more so in the island that was known
beyond all others as 'Little England', where, through all
colonial institutions, particularly church and school,
'English canons of beauty are taught and accepted even at
points where they are hostile to the self-respect of most
West Indians.'⁵

Blackman experienced this colonial assault on black
selfhood amid acute family poverty. In 1942 while taking
part in a BBC radio discussion entitled 'Home and Family
Life in the West Indies', he described the home conditions
of a young boy who, as well as his school work, labours in

the cane fields 'in order to supplement the family income. Nine years of age isn't too young for them to start.' He continued:

> Then the child goes home from school. He may be a bright boy and he's got a certain amount of homework to do, and he's got a tiny little lamp, 'snuff bottles' we used to call them at home. Well, imagine a boy working towards a scholarship or improving his mind, so to speak, in a little hut, say ten by fifteen feet perhaps, with a tiny partition in which his father and mother and three or four other children are living. You talk of fuel rationing here, but for us it's always limited. The boy had a very, very limited amount of kerosene – or paraffin, as you call it, by which to do his homework, or perhaps wants to work for two or three hours after dark, and his mother is thinking very much of how much longer that pint or half-pint of paraffin has got to last.

Blackman proved a successful student at Harrison College. He was particularly adept at languages and studied French and German as well as Latin and Greek, which prepared him well for the degree he took in Theology at the University of Durham, to which he won a scholarship, again through the intervention of the Anglican Church.

He became a priest himself and, in 1935, was sent to Gambia for missionary duties, but once he had arrived and settled into his post he discovered the stipend differentials between white and black clergy. Black missionaries were paid less and ranked lower than white. After unsuccessfully challenging the authorities over this racism, he resigned as a priest and returned to Barbados, only to emigrate again to Britain in 1937. Here he settled in London, throwing himself into West Indian politics-in-exile, joining the socialist-inclined Negro Welfare

Association and eventually becoming its Chair and a regular speaker. He became, too, an activist in the League of Coloured Peoples, was elected to its Executive Committee and, in 1938, became the editor of its journal, *The Keys*, writing powerful editorials on a wide range of political issues. In the same year, he worked with other Caribbean expatriates to establish the Committee for West Indian Affairs and became its Secretary, advising trade union leaders, lobbyists and left-leaning Members of Parliament on Caribbean issues to be raised in political debate in and outside the House of Commons. It was during this period that Blackman joined the Communist Party of Great Britain, then the sole UK party that called for independence for the colonies. Here he became an unpaid helper at the Party's London offices in Covent Garden, working on the *Colonial Information Bulletin*. Although he remained an active member before, through and after the 1939–45 war, he later asserted that it was because he was a *black* Communist that he had been excluded from any of the powerful committees and influential forums in the party; nor, despite his crucial and prominent roles in the broad spectrum of West Indian political organisations, did he have access to the CP leadership. Nonetheless, his writings openly drew from a Marxist analysis, which may have been why he was turned down when he sought to enlist into military service before the outbreak of war, although his skin colour was probably also a contributory factor. Throughout the war, though, he broadcast regularly on the BBC to the West Indies, while spending those years working on the assembly of Wellington bombers, eventually becoming a factory floor manager.

Afterwards, Blackman was virtually banned from the BBC because of the cold war. (Invaluable research by Joe Martin has revealed that his 'BBC File', which ended in 1954, was marked on its cover as 'politically suspect' and that all reference to the file must be taken to the 'CSA', whatever that was.)[6] But despite this labelling Blackman occasionally managed to achieve airtime, and get small amounts of pay for it too as a means of earning 'other oddments by way of funding a livelihood'. In 1942 he had given a talk '*Negro Writers*', including James Weldon Johnson, Claude McKay, Langston Hughes that was transmitted in the *Caribbean Voices* programme on the Colonial Service in May 1954. Yet in October of the same year a talk that he submitted about the African origins of Barbadian speech was rejected.

The attitudes of the BBC programme organisers to him were often hypocritical and hostile in their internal memos. One Godfrey James, who was responsible for book programmes, remarked that he felt that British listeners did not want to be 'howled at by those in distress' with material that was 'patently propaganda' or concerned itself with the 'colour bar'. Blackman's efforts to get his material accepted for BBC airtime were commented upon by a Mrs Horton of the Home Service: 'Poor P. Blackman. He keeps turning up and never quite enough, though nearly.'[7] Such remarks exemplified the attitudes which Blackman and his Caribbean contemporaries lived through and struggled against during their decades in London.

He continued to work as a skilled engineer for almost three decades. An engine fitter at Willesden Works, he was described by his wife as 'a nursemaid to steam engines'. An activist within the National Union of Railwaymen, he prided himself on being the only mechanic who knew both Latin and Greek, and he was strongly respected as a workmate who would help his companions with writing and literacy problems, frequently acting as a voluntary scribe and letter-writer. During this period he wrote for *Le Monde*, regularly travelling between London and Paris, as well as for the ground-breaking, negritude-influenced journal *Présence Africaine*. He was blacklisted and Special Branch security files were opened on his activities.

Many, many years later, in a talk organised by Art Against Racism and Fascism (AARF), Blackman spoke movingly of what the wartime experience and its aftermath had meant to him:

> German fascism, and what it meant in particular, threw us right back on our haunches and made us ashamed, in more ways than one, to be human ... [the poem] *My Song is for All Men* came out of actual experience. All my writing is what I call lived experience ... [I was on a visit] to the then unresurrected part of Warsaw which used to be called the Ghetto... there was a very distinguished English intellectual, Jewish by origin, the late Professor Levy. I remember walking with him through the Ghetto, a ... man of fifty, nearly sixty. He stooped down and picked up a torah, all bloodied over, and he turned his head away and I had to weep with him. Not because of the torah, but because he had been so hurt. He was a living representative of millions who had gone that way.[8]

The visit to Warsaw was an experience that cemented his political commitment to what he termed 'the extreme Left'. He went on, 'I remember saying to a friend, "Look, I don't agree with everything as you know. But after what I saw in Warsaw, if Harry Pollitt [then Secretary of the CPGB] were to kick me from one end of Oxford Street to the other, I would take it." For I would have nobody believe that the slightest fissure could be between me and the struggle against the filth that was fascism.'

During the postwar sojourns that Paul Robeson – loved and admired by ordinary people across the country – made in Britain, Blackman became his close companion. Blackman, who had become Robeson's friend before the war, organised Robeson's 1949 tour of Britain and travelled with him around Europe, including to Warsaw. And, with Robeson, he attended the World Peace Congress of 1949 in Paris, where he met W. E. B. DuBois. Blackman's son, also Peter, and himself a musician and drummer in the band *Steel and Skin,* remembered how his father travelled with Robeson to the Soviet Union. He recalled in conversation how Robeson would leave his possessions – like the woven bedspread from Nigeria or the African rug – at the Blackman family home in Heath Hurst Road, Hampstead, just a few doors away from where the poet Keats had once lived.

Discovering the poetry ...

I became a friend of Blackman relatively late in his life, during the mid-seventies, after I had read his long poem, *My Song is for All Men.* It had been reproduced in the journal *Black Liberator,* sold to me by one of its editors, Ricky Cambridge in 1973, during a demonstration in London. That demonstration was in support of Frelimo, the National Liberation Movement of Mozambique, where I went to teach in 1976-78 following national independence from Portuguese colonialism. Having been inspired by the poem, I managed to trace Blackman's whereabouts and frequently visited him at his basement flat in Belsize Park, where he lived alone. He was always warm and welcoming and we talked about many things. He told me that he had written a history of Africa which was still in manuscript form, that he had shown to several British historians of Africa, some of whom he accused of plagiarising it. He gave me too a copy of a long narrative poem which he referred to as 'Joseph', then unpublished and only partly typed. Moved by the poem, I invited him to my school in Poplar, East London, to read his work to my 14-year-old students. He was pleased to come, and sat in on several classes, talking genially to the students, who were of many different national origins, and reading extracts from his poems. He left me a copy of one short poem which he read, the unpublished and beautifully affectionate 'About London', so different from the long and very angry poem with a similar title that he had written in 1948:

> London I love for Johnson lingered there
> Donne preached and Blake saw God
> While Milton pondered man and God
>   his ways with man
> Have you ever heard the morning sing
> The morning sings with Blake
>
> I may walk at ease with these
> I shall walk in peace with these
> For they were first and always men
> Poets tireless to find some common
>   ground where men could meet
>
> This special image poets sought
> In special vision Blake once wrought
> To capture in simplicity
> The simple truth in you and me

By the summer of 1979, Blackman, now a septuagenarian, had agreed to speak at a poetry reading organised at the Half Moon Theatre, Stepney, East London, by Art Against Racism and Fascism. He was delighted to be there, in the old ex-synagogue, and in the unexpected company of his old contemporaries like the dockers' leader Jack Dash, who also read some of his poems, and the composer Alan Bush, who had put some of the lines of *My Song is for*

All Men together with extracts from Milton and Blake to music in his cantata *Voices of the Prophets* in 1952. Then, in April 1980, at the AARF meeting mentioned earlier, at which Blackman spoke of the events (including the visit to the Ghetto) that had prompted him to write *My Song is for All Men*, he read his poem *Stalingrad*. The audience was deeply affected. One of those present was the singer and ex-drummer of the jazz-rock band *Soft Machine*, Robert Wyatt, who was so moved that in the days after the reading he asked Blackman if he could record his rendition of *Stalingrad* and allow him to put it on the flipside of his next single record, a revival of the wartime anti-nazi song *Stalin wasn't Stallin*. The record was subsequently released in 1980, causing surprise, delight and some consternation despite Blackman's repudiation of Stalin and his brutal deformities (acknowledging, that during the decades since he had written Stalingrad and *My Song is for All Men* 'Stalin' had become 'a dirty word').[9] For Wyatt, the poem had expressed a resistance and joy that he felt compelled to hear time and time again. He later said: 'At a time of dramatically anti-establishment gestures, Peter Blackman's quiet, undemonstrative dignity as he crystallised key moments in our collective history, was a heartwarming revelation.'[10]

…and its qualities

What is it that makes Peter Blackman's poems so special, these works from a man from an illiterate small island family in the Eastern Caribbean? First, and above all, it is his huge grasp and knowledge of English, of Standard English – the language of his colonisers, which he saw as his one and only language. 'If I didn't speak English you might as well take the blood out of my veins, I have no other …I was drenched in some of the most beautiful English words from my childhood.'[11] And this despite his keen interest in the African origins of the Creole

Barbadian language spoken by his peers which was his own mother tongue, the theme of that rejected talk submitted to the BBC Third Programme series *A Question of Language* in October 1954. This was the language which Blackman's compatriot of the next generation, Edward Kamau Brathwaite, was to bring to poetic glory in his 'New World Trilogy' of *The Arrivants* in 1967-69. Blackman's virtual adoption by the Anglican church, his tutelage in an exclusive colonial school (like that of his Trinidadian contemporary, C.L.R. James) and his constant exposure to the King James Bible through his early years as his fundamental learning and literary text, pitched him inside a language context which, despite its reactionary history, he seized with imagination and brilliance. His extraordinary subsequent adaptation was the unique way he brought this colonial and ecclesiastical learning to a Marxist understanding of the world and a radiant hope and vision for its transformation.

With this he carried a quasi-religious idea of secular sainthood, which he invoked most strongly in *My Song is for All Men* in his descriptions of figures like his American friend Robeson, the Turkish communist poet Nazim Hikmet or, most starkly, the Czech anti-fascist and martyr murdered by the Nazis, Julius Fucik. In his Half Moon Theatre address, he spoke about meeting Fucik's wife:

> I remember the widow of Fucik describing to me her agony over her husband's death. We had great people among us and Fucik was one. People perhaps have never heard of him. I had only heard of him because I went to Czechoslovakia. But I have always felt that what we want, and I say 'we' meaning the Left because I still regard the Left as the spearhead of progress in the world, wherever it is – I think we need to find categories of reference which will mean as much to us and to subsequent generations as, for instance, the

Christians use their saints. They have their St. John and St. James, their St. Mary who are standing for this and that. We have got enough heroes and people – but we needn't call them heroes because that implies something objectionable.[12]

Such people, continued Blackman – and he extends his theme in his AARF Garage Theatre address – were the 'ordinary people', those 'who go to work every day' and produce excellence. 'It doesn't matter what they do. They could be newspapermen, they could sweep the streets. Out of them comes excellence'. He invoked the 'people of France' who resisted Nazi occupation, 'the countless people who did not stand up to be counted, they just *stood up*, and because they stood up they were counted and the enemy took them away to unspeakable tortures which none of us knew about and few of us, even today, like to think about. It is out of that living that comes, not the big shout, not the name in the headlines. The quiet man who just stays there – he makes the world *human*. That is the man, and the woman, that I want to see sung, talked about in poetry and in literature.'[13] 'What we must try and do is get at the ordinary, and so work that without any suspicion of deterioration .. out of the ordinary .. we bring excellence, without elitism.'[14] And these are all those 'ordinary' human beings all over the world that he celebrates in his poems, particularly in *My Song is for All Men*.

Then there is 'Stalingrad', an astonishing poem in its scope and an eloquent forerunner to the equally cosmic vision of *My Song is for All Men*. What Stalingrad stood for, said Blackman, quoting Wordsworth's paean to Toussaint l'Ouverture, was 'man's unconquerable mind'. In inception, conception and execution, it is a poem that renders tangible the internationalism of humanity that is the core of Blackman's work. Written by a man from a

Caribbean island with a tiny population, it was dedicated to the courage of a distant people who had turned back the most powerful army on Earth; who, even in Churchill's estimation, 'tore the guts out of the Nazi war machine', and who lost 20 million men and women in the process. Blackman tells how the world's people responded to the epochal victory of Stalingrad, from South African miners to English housewives, from Argentinian gauchos to Canadian trappers and the incarcerated of Belsen. A praisesong of human joy and hope, it is so unlike most contemporary postmodernist and introverted poetic utterance of now-times, as to be almost another language at work entirely.

Blackman's narrative of the centre of empire, telling 'the tale of the Empire red with blood' in his 1948 poem 'London' is profoundly different to that (quoted earlier) written almost three decades later about the post-imperial city which he read to classes of young and cosmopolitan East Londoners in 1976. That earlier 'London' is a hellish, ugly and vicious city, its population a 'bastard brood' cursed within 'a tangle of strange meannesses' which erupts in the telling of a seemingly autobiographical incident when a housedog-loving landlady

> Could find no lodgement from the madness
> For a woman and her unborn child
> Since both were black

Indeed, considering such neighbours as her, the poet mourns that 'I shared breathing with them', mean-spirited and racist as they were, and sees an 'accounting' coming closer for them as 'the peoples rise, like seas, tumultuous' in a revolutionary future.

Blackman's apex of known utterance is, however, *My Song is for All Men*, published as a pamphlet in both London

and New York in 1952 by the Communist Party publishers
Lawrence and Wishart, during the zenith of the Cold War.
This was, in particular the period of conflict in Korea,
little remembered today, which resulted in 4 million
Korean casualties, involved upwards of 300,000 US
soldiers at the time of the armistice in July 1953, as well as
thousands more British military regulars and national
servicemen. The poem is partly a prophetic treatise in
which the poet declares that he 'must state a case for the
black man', anticipating many a black power and black
consciousness affirmation of two decades later; and partly
a lovesong for all humanity, particularly its working
people – all the 'ordinary' people of the world. 'Look this
is a white hand,' he declares, 'it is my hand, I am the black
man.' Its references to places in all continents are like an
index to a world atlas and its salutes to workers
everywhere know no bounds. These humans are the
'Leaves of Grass' invoked by Walt Whitman, and
Blackman's love for the 'loafing' poet of America becomes
powerfully explicit here. Whitman, we are told, composed
his long-lined verses while sitting on the beaches of Long
Island as the waves hurled themselves against the shore-
line, and I have often imagined the Barbadian boy
Blackman, hearing similar rhythms as the Atlantic waves
crashed against the long and rocky Bathsheba Beach on
his own island. Certainly there are many echoes of
Whitman and his versification in both form and theme in
My Song is for All Men.

The war in Korea is directly referenced in the poem, as
Blackman's empathy rises for the US 'Negro bomb aimer'
spreading fire, havoc and poison from his aircraft to kill
Koreans and destroy their harvests, while thinking
simultaneously about the plight of his own sharecropping
family and their cotton in Georgia, 'red as the napalm
drenched with the blood of his father, Burnt the same day
he was drafted'. It is a direct pointer to the Vietnam

conflict which deformed the lives of the next generation of young Americans as well as millions of Vietnamese.

The poem's climax and portraiture of the world's children – German, African, Kamchatchuan, Georgian and Japanese – held together by the poet's love, is close to a vision of Blake. It is welded by a daring contemporary image of nuclear fission, with an atomic blast used positively to express the overwhelming power of a universal love and solidarity that ends forever all 'the evil oppression which cripples all our creation.' It is an image which could only have been grasped and used by the poet in his time, before the world of the anti-nuclear movement would have rendered it repugnant, and he employs it with an extraordinary potency to complete his poem.

I have often wondered whether the long narrative poem 'Joseph' is in fact unfinished, although when Blackman gave it to me, it was offered as a completed work. I believe that it was written at some time during the late 1950s as a deliberate act of literary solidarity with the US Civil Rights movement and its brave resistance to established racism in the states of Mississippi and Alabama. The poem's final ironic line: 'THESE THINGS OF COURSE COULD NOT HAPPEN IN ENGLAND' seems strangely at odds with some of the poem's standout English archaisms, with Joseph the black servant described as 'a young and bonny gaillard' or his white mistress portrayed as a woman who is 'unflecked by wantonness', but as a versified story of vicious racism and hypocritical dealings, it shows how this could, of course, flourish within British social life.

This collection's final poem is a tribute to the life, work and dreams of Claudia Jones. A comrade to Blackman of the aspiring Caribbean nation, she was born in Trinidad in 1915, and in 1922 she moved to New York with her three sisters to join her mother, a garment worker, and her father (a former newspaper editor in his home country) who was an apartment superintendent. Claudia, inspired by the Communist Party's work in campaigning for the freedom of the Scottsboro' Boys, joined the Young Communist League in 1936 and became an associate editor of its journal, the *Weekly Review* and, during the war, editor of its monthly *Spotlight*. Because of her work and postwar agitation for the CPUSA, particularly her organising against the war in Korea she was regularly harassed and arrested, and by the early 1950s had begun to suffer serious heart disease. In 1955 she was deported to Britain. Her comrade, Elizabeth Gurley Flynn, wrote a farewell poem for her, anticipating Blackman's tribute, which included this stanza:

> No more to see you striding down the pathway,
> No more to see your smiling eyes and radiant face.
> No more to hear your gay and pealing laughter,
> No more enriched by your love, in this sad place.[15]

The non-stop activism of Claudia's decade in London, which included founding and editing the pioneering black journal *West Indian Gazette*, her oppositional work against the racist overtones of the 1962 Immigration Act, her building of solidarity for anti-colonial movements in Asia, Africa and her own Caribbean nation, her involvement in struggles against fascist and racist violence in London's Notting Hill neighbourhood and her part in creating the Notting Hill Carnival, ended with her penniless death in a freezing North London flat on Christmas Eve, 1964. Blackman's poem to her is a reflection of that hard and brave London decade that he experienced too, and her life, like those of Fucik, Robeson or Hikmet, was that of an exemplary human being. His compatriot, the Barbadian novelist George Lamming, who like Blackman used his English words as beautifully and skillfully as the greatest of English writers, said of her, at the same February 1965 memorial meeting at St. Pancras Town Hall, London, at which Blackman read his poem to Claudia:

> Politics resided in every nerve of Claudia's body. Militant for her cause, she was also generous in her relationships. The lioness could disagree like an angel. Here was a great source of her strength; a certain flexibility of mind and a generous heart.[16]

Blackman's words to her are, too, the expression of his deepest creed:

> She said
> I walk with the humble
> Yet not in humility
> We scale the winds
> My feet shall be
> No swifter than their feet
> My limbs shall share
> No strength that is not theirs
> When we move we move mountains

***

After months of thought, decisions, counter-decisions and text-searching I decided to call this brief collection *Footprints*. Blackman, midway through *My Song is for All Men*, declares that the black man's and woman's 'footprints are nowhere in history', a statement which must now be read with irony. I also had fast in my mind the tune composed by the great American jazz tenor saxophonist Wayne Shorter, included first on his 1966 classic Blue Note album, *Adam's Apple*, with pianist Herbie Hancock, bassist Reggie Workman and drummer Joe Chambers, like Blackman, four black humans making their indelible marks on the future. I think Blackman would have loved and relished their sounds.

These few surviving poems of Blackman are enough to profile him as a major Caribbean poet. Their uniqueness, beauty and human vision surge from the midst of the struggles and injustices of the era within which he lived as statements of brave literary, social and political resistance. My abiding hope is that the rest of his works, more of his poetry, history and commentary will also be recovered and published one day, so that future generations, black and white, will read and know his powerful revolutionary testimony, from the Caribbean, through Africa to London and beyond.

Chris Searle
Sheffield, November 2012

References

[1] Trevor Carter, *Shattering Illusions: West Indians in British politics* (London, Lawrence and Wishart, 1986).
[2] E.K. Brathwaite, *History of the Voice* London, New Beacon Books, 1984).
[3] Peter Blackman, 'Address to a meeting organised by Art Against Racism and Fascism', 1980.
[4] Peter Blackman, 'Is there a West Indian literature?', *Life and Letters* (London, 1948).
[5] *Ibid*.
[6] From research notes of Joe Martin, taken from personal file on Peter Blackman at the BBC.
[7] *Ibid*.
[8] Peter Blackman, address to a meeting organised by Art against Racism and Fascism, 13 April 1980, Garage Young People's Theatre, Sloane Square, London.

[9] *Ibid.*

[10] Robert Wyatt, in correspondence with Chris Searle, November 2012.

[11] Blackman, AARF address, 1980, op. cit.

[12] From tape of Peter Blackman's address to an Art Against Racism and Fascism meeting at the Half Moon Theatre, November 1979.

[13] *Ibid.*

[14] Blackman, AARF address, 1980, op. cit.

[15] Quoted in Clara West, 'Claudia Jones: a life in struggle', 11 February 2007, http://www.politicalaffairs.net/claudia-jones-a-life-in-the-struggle/

[16] George Lamming, 'We mourn her to celebrate her example', *West Indian Gazette* (Vol. 8, no. 2, February 1965).

Stalingrad

Hushed was the world and o dark agony that suspense
shook upon us
While hate came flooding o'er your wide savannahs
Plunging pestilence against you all that stood to state
That where men meet there meets one human race

Therefore did men from Moscow to the Arctic
Rounding Vladivostock south where Kasbek lifts its peak
Still work and working waited news of Stalingrad

> And from Cape to wide Sahara men asked news of
> Stalingrad
> Town and village waited what had come of
> Stalingrad
> The tom-tom beat across thick forest while every
> evening at palaver

> Old men told of Stalingrad
> The gauchos caught the pampas whisper
> Wind swept hope of Stalingrad
> And in the far Canadian north
> Trappers left their baiting for the latest out of
> Stalingrad

> In the factories and coalfields each shift waited
> What last had come from Stalingrad
> While statesmen searched the dispatch boxes
> What they brought of Stalingrad

> And women stopped at housework held their
> children close to hear
> What was afoot at Stalingrad
> For well man knew that there a thousand years
> was thrown the fate of the peoples

Stalingrad o star of glory
Star of hope o star of flame
O what a midwife for this glory
Take for the pattern Pavlov and his men
A Soviet soldier and his nine companions
Who full seven weeks sleepless by night and day
Fought nor gave ground
They knew that with them lay
That where men meet should meet one human race

Carpenters who had built houses wanted only to build
more
Painters who still painted pictures wanted only to
paint more
Men who sang life strong in laughter wanted only to
sing more
Men who planted wheat and cotton wanted only to
plant more
Men who set the years in freedom sure they would be
slaves no more
They spoke peace to their neighbours at tilling
For in peace they would eat their bread
Uzbeks, Tatars, Letts, Ukrainians, Russians,
Muscovites, Armenians
Who ringed forests wide round Arctic
Brought sands to blossom tundras dressed for spring
These kept faith in Stalin's town
We may not weep for those who silent now rest here
Garland these graves
These lives have garlanded
All our remaining days with hope
Stalingrad o star of glory
Star of hope here spread your flame

Now when news broke
That Stalingrad still lived upon the banks of Volga
That Stalingrad was still a Soviet town
Then the turner flung his lathe light as a bird
And the gaucho spread his riot in the pampas
For this news of Stalingrad
The tom-tom beat wild madness when the elders
brought palaver
These tidings out of Stalingrad
The English housewife stopped her housework held
her child close
And cried aloud now all men will be free
And from Good Hope black miners answered
This will help us to be free
In the prison camps of Belsen sick men routed
from their guards
Now life was certain soon all men would be free
New light broke upon Africa new strength for her
peoples
New strength poured upon Asia new hope for
her peoples
America dreamed new dreams from the strength of
her peoples
New men arose in Europe new force for her peoples
Once more they stand these men at lathe and spindle
To recreate their hours and each new day
Did houses rise once more in Soviet country
Men ring forests wide round Arctic
Move rivers into deserts
And with high courage breed new generations
For still the land is theirs
Uzbeks, Tatars, Letts, Armenians
Caucasians, Muscovites, Crimeans
Still they speak peace to their neighbours at tilling
To all the wide world
And men come near to listen
Find by that day of Stalingrad
This voice is theirs

Then Red star spread your flame upon me
For in your flame is earnest of my freedom
Now may I rendezvous with the world
Now may I joy in man's wide-flung diversity
For Stalingrad is still a Soviet town.

London

I
Stand here and watch
The tidal waves of human lives
Converging
From every shore;
Crowds
Sour as water stagnant
In a Fenland,
Never moved to laughter
Save at others' hurt;
The deep repulsion of strange vivid strengths recoiling
From the shock of meeting;
Out of this turmoil I was born.

I am London.
These fashion me
As I am;
Beget upon me
Strange imaginings;
The lone mirages
of outraged virginity
Seeking resolution.
These are my children.
Daily
The bastard brood
Defile me,
Turning inward
For their delight.
Come, I will show them,
Each to his thought,
His speech each to his power.

Marvel not
At the strangeness of my creations,
Many men have ploughed upon my field,
All paid and stayed
The while they could,
None wooed for long.
It was not that I loved them,
It was not that pleasure with them
I could either take or give;
They served, and in their strength
I grew to majesty.

II

Came a maid
Of wondrous beauty,
Formed as of quivering bronze.
Her kinship owed
Rebellion rude
Of several bloods;
She passed, and passed thus brooding:
All men revile me,
All deny me
Right of kinship in their halls;
Sum in me
The vices of the nations.
Hate sits in my bones,
The vengeful hate of conquest
Was rudely uttered
In the caresses of my father
When he begat me.
My mother,
Bruised and broken
Wept,
Frenzied by his embraces
When she conceived me,
Delight in every tendon,
Hatred in her heart.

I am a woman of sorrows
And acquainted with grief,
The Painted Whore.
Not Rome,
Nor Babylon,
Nor modern counterpart of each –
Paris, New York, or London,
But flesh and blood
Daughter of man's strength,
Usufruct of marriage
Named a child,
Yvonne, Juliette, or Maude.
The Bitch within the skin
Some call me,
Others, Magdalene.
These last are they
Whose God cohabits virginwards
Leaving to lesser loins
The summing of the Zone's now broken total;
A wider choice from censure free
Below the salt.
Yet these and those alike
A thousand hells have harboured in my loins,
Have used, devoured, and scorned,
And cooled a thousand red-hot passions in the floods
Of my physical consenting.

She spake,
The bitter tear thrust inward
Like a pearl;
The flesh all faulted,
Born to brilliance
Out of agony.

III

Steel upon steel,
Mile upon mile of grey girders,
Telegraph poles
Swift with wind murmurs –
The Colossus spans the world,
Clay for the feet,
Gold for the heart and the head,
Sawdust embrazened.
Fearful looms
The new Moloch
Seeking with passionate hate
For the pulse of the life-flow;
The soul, the heart and the bones
Of men to bestride.
Sawdust embrazened,
Clanging steel upon steel,
Mile upon mile of grey girders,
Telegraph poles
Swift with wind murmurs,
Gold for the heart and the head,
And clay for the feet.

IV

How like a morsel harried forth of hell
The tenement stands
In grim abandon of ruinous dance with death.
Death steps here, but not with dignity.

Imperial people,
Still runs the tale of Empire red with blood.
Rear the mausoleum,
Trail the hearse
Hung o'er with tasselled guilt of many another life.
Death steps here, but not with dignity.

Frustrated rage, vicarious, deadly,
Passions embattled in grim deed undone
Crave blood for atonement.
Death steps here, but not with dignity.

Flesh must weep, where flesh is broken.
Then flood the waters,
Cut deep the sabre-edge of Hate,
The pattern wrest e'en from the body's roots,
Nor let shrewd afterthought of love save Noah from death
To recreate this form
In other worlds of life.
Here Death steps.

V

I have seen a people cursed,
Cursed by its own too much desire,
Life made a tangle of strange meannesses
Miscalled ambition.

Grey masks in the dusk
Their leprous faces front me darkling,
Full of hate.
Fearful hate,
Spawn of hot-headed rivalry,
Kindred in meannesses.
Millions, so many;
Bodies sprawling earthwards,
Million bodies soon fragmented into dust,
Bodies mating deathly with steel splinters.
God, contemplating these despaired of Hell.

I stand amid the blood, fear, and confusion,
Silent.
I feel not for these bodies,
I cannot mourn these bodies.

This one had peddled all her love to a little Chinese dog,
Had fed him tid-bits while little children starved,
This one, the one who sent my wife in tearful humiliation
        from her door.
My wife was big with child;
Bigger the tears this hurt brought to her eyes.
This one, the one who lodged the little Chinese dog,
Could find no lodgement from the madness round
For a woman and her unborn child,
Since both were black.

Now she too lies in tid-bits
Spurned even by the little Chinese dog.
I feel not for these bodies,
I cannot love these bodies,
I mourn not these bodies.

In other days I might have mourned
That I shared breathing with them.
In other years I feared to share
The Resurrection with them.
Now fears are fled;
I share
The wide world with them.
Here I shall gain a standing for my manhood,
With them, or despite them;
Shall always beat down those who still would parley with
        them.

VI

The tumult and the shouting rise
To mad crescendo.
Priapus stalks abroad
The phallus humorous.
Damsels inventive stand
Inviting union.
Whom shall we have for unsung hero
On the eleventh day of the next eleventh month?
In his eleventh year, this child?
The bombs drop, the thrushes pipe their praise
In still, small voice,
Unheard.

I came to my people,
My people wept
And found no comfort
Throughout long joyless days and nights of sudden terror.
Ye prophets and ye lying ones,
When will ye speak a language understanded of the people?
I brought her daffodils, white daffodils.
She said, 'Bring no more daffodils, white daffodils;
Their odour is too much of death for these days.'
Flowers, withering under threat of dissolution,
All creeds are outmoded. There is no stay.

VII

Weep not beloved,
Or, if weep you must,
Weep unashamedly
And 'suage the soaring passion of your heart,
Lest suddenly
The torment rend you
And leave you less than man.

Not with Pilate
Lies the need on you
To proffer clean-washed hands
To emphasize your separateness from guilt,
That Rachel weeping for her children
Will not find them here.
They died in Barcelona,
Shanghai, Addis Ababa,
This full seven year.

Friends then with Nero fiddled while Rome burned;
They watched the human sink beneath the symbol,
Bade women rot and stalwart men decay,
Children still unseeded in them.
Now Nero stands
Amid his stagnant puddle
Frantic in passion, mocked by skies that will not give him ear,
And so to stoop
More than one half patched and palsied
To gather fragments of a broken life.

Still they pass by,
Ghosts

Insubstantial pageants
Compounded all of air,
Thin air.
So they earn wages,
Token of the life to come.
Bread is to-morrow.
Or the grave.

Let us now praise famous men,
Those who forbid us thought of resurrection.
There is no vision,
Here the people perish.

VIII

Here is no place for cryptic phrasing,
Here is not time for hidden meaning,
The word must shape its senses plainly or we die.
When simian madness shatters all foundations
Men must tame brutes.

Let cowards shrink,
Let traitor phantoms cry How long Lord!
Who will stand by
All sicklied o'er with fear,
Those let the deluge take,
Such we can spare.
Doubts infantine, hesitation,
Can here find no place.
Now must our passion be translated
Into the idiom of force.
The men we hate will choose our living,
Or we forestall them.

The peoples rise, like seas, tumultuous;
Come, ride the flood!
The peoples rise, like seas, tumultuous,
Come, ride the flood,
Ere 'twixt high tide and ebb the power dies.
The fight is fierce;
Chance of battle falls to none
Who dare not bravely lead;
Speak, those who know.

Comes the accounting.
Will you then say that others wrought this shame?
Of you and your strength is this murder all compounded,
From you and your strength only comes its end.

The peoples rise, like seas, tumultuous.
No runic charm will incantate this flood,
Here no mystery, here no gods,
These are men
Of bodies, parts, and passions
To clear purpose welded.
Let those who say that 'we are gods'
Beware the madness of the people.

My Song is for All Men

I

My song is for all men Jew Greek Russian
Communist pagan Christian Hindu Muslim Pole Parsee
And since my song is for all men
More than most I must state a case for the black man.

I have wandered with the Men of Devon over the Devon hills
Conned thought with Milton where low voices drift
through time buoying music over death and forgetfulness
I have wandered beyond to distant Caucasia
Skirting my wonder of blood wined in the beauty
Of green mountains hemmed by blue waters on Georgia's coast
I have listened to debate in London and Moscow
Prague Paris and many another town
I have heard statement confused or insistent
patient or fretted facing a claim
And ever the claim was the same
"This is my own" the voices repeated "my hands have built it.
           It is my very own. Show us your fruiting."
Let me then bring mine own
This is mine own. I state a claim for the black man

I am the black man
I hide with pigmies in the hot depth of the forest that is Africa's
                                                              girdle
I am the Zulu striding hot storm over the brown whispering
                                                              veldt
that rides in my blood like a battle
I am the Ashanti I fold my strength in the beaten gold
of a stool shaped for immortals
I am the Nilotic standing one-legged for my rest
I am the Hyskos escaped out of Egypt and become king of Ruandi
I am the miner baring the wealth of South Africa
I hold the fate of the world in my hands in the uranium pits of
                                                         the Congo
I am no more the man of Zambesi than I am the man of Limpopo
I am no less the man from the mountains of Kavirondo than I am

                              the warrior bred of the Masai
I am as much Ibo as I am Yoruba
I am all that is Africa I reach out to embrace those who have
                                        left me
I dig cane-holes in hot West Indian islands
I run donkeyman on trampships plying from Cardiff
I wear a red cap on all North American railroad stations

I bring rough hands calloused in the tumult of weariness
Strong-boned not given to prayer force strained to hard bruising
Bearing rough burdens to enrich men in England America
                  France Holland Brazil. I work for my bread.

A woman comes with me long-limbed high-bosomed proud of
                                        countenance
She walks abroad her presence dressed
Fluent of Earth and love
Sweet as the fresh-rained corn at early morning

Eyes soft as mountain lakes deep-shaded
O'er shot of sunshine truant midst the reeds
At hide and seek with laughter supply flung
The music of her motion

Sweeter is this purple grape
Than Pompadour's wild roses
Wide-eddied leaps life's promise
Strong
In the rivers of her keeping

The Black woman brings her beauty
I shall sing it
Bid every nation know
And worship it
With her at my side I measure all things
She is the source of my pride from her stem all my creations

II

And since there are those who pretend to estimate the peoples
Sum and divide them to suit the needs of their policy
That for this class, this for that superior nation,
Shaped and assessed on the rate of their own order in merit
There are some things I must say to them

And oh men of Europe Asia America and all the sea islands
Come near and look at these faces
For this also concerns you
And you men of Africa especially scan them well and remember
them
You will find them to-day
In London Paris New York Buenos Aires Madrid and Berlin
One and all for themselves very superior persons
The Bitch of Belsen too was a very superior person
She was for herself a fine humanist held a peculiar conception
Of art, she loved dogs had a taste highly refined above others for
parchment
The skin of a painter musician a giant tattooed
Some poet greater than these to sing the strength of the peoples
Alone could suffice her for lampshades
She too shared our shape
She knew her man carnally kissed him caressed him longed for
him utterly when the need was upon her
As would a bitch for her dog? no she was at every point woman
And around herself and her living she wove a beastly deception

There are many like her in our world let us never forget them
Let us examine them
Swear with me here on oath that these will no longer govern
our world

These are the men who find my presence constraining in Alabama
Barbados London Texas and similar places
They teach their children to turn their faces away when they see
me

They say my features are coarse and repulsive
Too like the ape for man. Against these I have always to argue
                                              my humanity

I may not travel in cabins on shipboard with them
Nor sit at table with them command them in armies or navies
                        in churches pray with them or for them
In Johannesburg their child if his skin be white
May push me from his path on the sidewalk
And as he feels his strength increasing to manhood
He may kick me into the gutter. No law bring me redress
They would have me stand in their polity one for whom laws are
                        made not one who may make them
My part to obey and to serve hew wood and draw water
I am expected to stand respectfully bared while this kind talk
                                                        to me
Crawl cringe and dance like a poodle trained to beg crusts or a
                                              bone for amusement

At Martinsville in the United States of America they hanged me
on the word of a white prostitute hot from the stews
Where all night long she fretted her pennies
Prone till the morning taught her lost virtue
The source of its pride when she saw me
No one could prove my guilt there was none to be proven
The judge simply stated my death would have a wholesome effect
                                              on the community
So they burnt me at Richmond in the name of Christ and
                                              democracy
To smother the fears that shook them as they played at a race
                                              of the masters.

To all my wide continent I welcomed these they came to Africa
seized all they could lay hands upon
Took the best lands for their tilling to build them white houses
I pass them each day cool deep-shaded in green
Their dwelling places wanton in lovelinesses
Spread for their senses by sky river and sea

I shelter my weariness in old packing cases
Cast of their luxury offscourings of cardboard and tin
Scraped of their surfeit too mean to cover their dog
My nakedness is whipped from sleep by rain pouring
at midnight to strip me in torment the last space
Earth pledged safe from their craving
To these I have something to say

These you claim are only my just deservings
Rags and old packing cases fair receivings
For beasts such as I am so you say
Crabbed you would tent me manacled as madmen
Once crouched beneath your palaces
I am unlearned in philosophies of government
I may not govern myself children must learn of their elders
till they are elders themselves
I know nothing of science never created a great civilisation
Poetry song music sculpture are alike foreign to my conceiving

I have never built a monument higher than a mudhut
Nor woven a covering for my body other than the passing leaves
of the grass

I am the subman
My footprints are nowhere in history

This is your statement, remember, this your assessment
I merely repeat you
Remember this too, I do not ask you to pity me
Remember this always you cannot condescend to me

There are many other things I remember and would have you
remember as well
I smelted iron in Nubia when your generations still ploughed
with hardwood
I cast in bronze at Benin when London was marshland
I built Timbuctoo and made it a refuge for learning
When in the choirs of Oxford unlettered monks shivered
unwashed

My faith in the living mounts like a flame in my story
I am Khama the Great
I helped Bolivar enfranchise the Americas
I am Omar and his thousands who brought Spain in the light of the
Prophet
I stood with my spear among the ranks of the Prempehs
And drove you far from Kumasi for more than a century
I kept you out of my coasts and not the mosquitoes
I have won many bitter battles against you and shall win them
again
I am Toussaint who taught France there was no limit to liberty
I am Harriet Tubman flouting your torture to assert my faith in
man's freedom
I am Nat Turner whose daring and strength always defied you
I have my yesterdays and shall open the future widely before me

I am Paul Robeson
I send out my voice and fold peoples warmly to my bosom
I sow courage in myriad bleak places where it is grown worn
My song kept this fire alight in the fiords of Norway under the
Nazis
for my power is never diminished
I pile volcanoes in the minds of Mississippi sharecroppers
I engage continents
Beyond all bars you set I shall reach out
To tear life's glory down I shall reach out
To set life's crown upon mine own head with mine own hand
Shall reach out and never forget the reckoning

But first I must separate myself from your every particular
I must touch you at no point
I must shun your very fringes
And in all my living I shall never be alone

III

I know you of old your hatred of men
How you sour the earth with this hate
How you trap men and twist them, plant fear like a plague
                                                      between them

The hatred you turn against me I have seen repeated in savagery
Ten thousand times in ten thousand different places
A whole world rises against you a whole world whose living
Warped in your footsteps can only be safe at your death
Let us then dress the bill of your crimes let us examine them

A young man stands at the street corner in Paris
Stripping life's need in the pitiless reach of a prostitute
Tenting love's flower in a rough waste of deception
All life's power maimed in a snare of francs pennies and dimes
                                                      you spread for him

The Malayan father gathers his dead from a thicket
A child of ten years disfigured and charred by flame-throwers
The soldier who stifled his laughter bartered his hunger at the
                                        rate of two shillings a day
For God justice and fatherland lies you crudely exchanged for
                                                      his need

The dead still stand in the Valleys of Korea old men and women
burnt alive with the harvest by napalm
A child hides his loneliness stark in a blanket of snow by the
                                        roadside at Seoul
I sit with the Negro bomb-aimer who set them alight
I hear his heart weep blind in an anguish of torment as he set
                                                      the release
His mind bright with the thought of the cotton in Georgia
Red as the napalm drenched with the blood of his father
Burnt the same day he was drafted

I was thrown a live bomb into the sea around Madagascar
My scream echoed the child's which outtopped the flames
                                    roaring at Oradour
I plunged deep as the hell in the mind of the child's father who
                                    sent me to death

In Auschwitz Belsen and Buchenwald
Your fury put off its disguise
Here you stood plain as a murderer
You prided yourself in your trade

You school your pride in the fruits of other men's labour
Pile stone upon stone monumented a thousand feet skyward
Trace swifter than Puck a girdle for earth
And in Hiroshima drive the blistering sands anguished in last
                                    tears
For human eyes rained liquid in the dust at your compelling
My very blood disdains you
I am all that is human
I raise my voice million-headed in the market places
Where I wrestle the sun to my living
I serve you due notice
I shall not enter death's overmastering silence
A slave at your bidding
I bring my might to forestall you
I write this pledge with my blood thus of my heart's core
                                    compelled me
Strong in the assurance of my own reality
I shall keep faith with the living

My case is not framed for plaintive complaining
Strong anger is knotted to my every desire
Bathing my limbs and refreshing the promises
Made for the reckoning
You will remember the reckoning

I shall forget nothing
I lay it all to your account
I shall forgive nothing
I shall not mime with withered fingers
In the days not far off when we measure our strength

IV

The account has already been rendered many a payment been
made
Over the years I hear strong voices rise from the springtime of
our living

Let me here gather the force of Julius Fucik
Last heard of in Pankrats in Prague
'Old men who have spent the sum of their strength
Know when the time is come to greet death and go with him
But my strength is at noon the sun of my life nowhere near
setting
Warm blood flows over my muscles many a morning sings yet in
my heart

My one wish is to stay with the living
But I shall die soon, for the men with me here have only for
thought how to kill me
Tomorrow the sun will rise and I shall not see it
The walls will be warm but not for my touch
Yet I fear only one death that in my pain my class be betrayed
So let me hold fast to my class let its million strengths strengthen
me

I live while my class lives at my death it continues
Then Nazis know you can never destroy me
Tomorrow my flesh will be dust your hangmen's hands are well
fashioned to kill me
But my fight will be lived again in lands I have never seen
Argentine Nigeria southmost down earth to Tierra del Fuego
Far past Good Hope in West Indies China Korea among the
Laplanders

Deep in my own Czechoslovakia
Though I shall not see with these eyes the hopes that will spring
from this sowing
I know earth will be gay with the harvest men will live and love
one another
The good men the strong men the true men the working men
They will take account of your kind they will root them out
utterly

Today you are absolute I do not accept you
Now hack me in pieces I shall not whisper
Uproot my tongue my silence defeats you
And oh men remember remember I loved you
The good men the true men the strong men the working men
You whose sweat is your daily bread
Whose strength is your class
Together we shall keep faith with the living.'

Over the years a strong voice rises
An eagle swoops in the sun

The sunlight flecks the gold of his crest and song carries on
I too Julius I know your sorrow and the tale of your glory
I am Nazim Hikmet I stand astride Europe and Asia I judge
                                                    them both
I look toward Africa I hold the world in the palm of my hand
I walk with the lowliest I speak for them
For this the men who misgovern my country put me in prison

Many things come to me here in my cell many things
Love most and the warmth of my fellows
My courage thrusts far beyond Anatolia to all the wide earth
Time is a friend which brings millions to speak with me
I listen I have had long to listen
By twilight at noon while moonlight crept my only companion
                                                    soft to my pillow
Sometimes all night I kept vigil with men stripped of their flesh
by pitiless hunger in the prison camps of the Nazis
I had heard this hunger sobbing before in the wide weary eyes
                                                    of children
In Oldham West Indies Africa London wreathing dead skins
                                                    round high harvest
In Ireland India China
That those who despise our humanity should add ten more per
                                                    cent to their dividends
These things happened then not behind the curtain of war

But in the times they name peace in the streets on the farms
Among the sharecroppers white and black in Virginia
Glad to fill their bellies with earth when the factor had stolen
                                        their maize and their cotton
Among the poor whites and the Zulus coloureds and Hottentots
                                        who live at the Cape
Among the sun-browned fields of Missouri where they ploughed
                                        back the corn
Because those who planted it had no money to buy it
In Grimsby where they gave the night's catch back to the sea
For men may not eat fish when they have no money to buy it
In Brazil where they fed the coffee as fuel to engines
In Argentine as they slaughtered the cattle since millions in China
Shall not eat flesh because they have no money to buy it
In Belsen Auschwitz Buchenwald the murder was somewhat
                                        more ordered
Vastness was all, gas but the sign of a superior civilisation

Oh men of Europe Africa Asia America Australia and all the
                                        sea islands
These men feed on our flesh like a cancer
War is but the end of their logic
Let us then dress the bill of our claims let us examine them
Comrades and friends it is to you I am speaking not to the others

I know all your sorrow brothers the years have revealed it
My flesh winced as the rough horse-hide stripped Zoya naked
The rude sjambok tearing a Zulu in Orange Free State
Still wakes my sleep in a nightmare
On my heart is a rose a red rose a whole land scarleted courage
For the roses are red in Korea all the earth is a rose staunched
                                        in the blood of its people
Red as the star that shall sit in the triumph this people will win

Let us then dress the bill of our claims let us dress them confidently
For the shouts of the battle rise a roar of wild waters
Crying triumph at Stalingrad

A fury of anger floods madly through China sweeping corruption
swift to the sea
All round me thunder the peasants loud throated greeting the
soldiers
They have come a long march all the days of the year over high
mountains
To bring us this peace
Their feet are bright on the hillside bivouacking the morning

From Paris Morocco Alaska Calcutta the echoes come back to
batter the door of my prison
Brown hands black hands white hands yellow hands
Flatten the walls of my cell
Now I go into the daylight to continue my song, my song this
strong hope
The pledge that today we shall live the assurance of all our
tomorrows
Here the one chant we may raise at this time
For the men of our class for their joy in their living
Their courage wherever we find them

And you Julius, Zoya, Danielle, Peri
You with the thousands known to us the thousands whose names
are denied us
I greet as I go forth to the morning free because you kept faith
I go like you to keep faith with the living

Over the years strong voices rise
from the springtime of our living

And I the black poet I answer these voices
For these voices are mine
I may not forget these though oceans divide us
For their sorrow is child of my sorrow my pain is their pain
My joy theirs to rejoice in, their song my remembrancer
I sing as I bind the stoops in the cane fields of Cuba
Where I hew out the gold at the Cape or the coal in Virginia

See the morning is bright our strength opens the gate of
                                                    tomorrow

Let me then name them let me remember them here let me
                                                    praise them
Those who have lent light to my living
Rising a chorus comes with them Jan Drda spent like a fountain
                                                    of merriment
Emi Siao lending soft kindness to all who come near him
Pablo Neruda vast as the Andes bordering every horizon
They come with their peoples of Asia Europe and all the Americas

With them also I remember with praise
All who alike individually and in thought banded together share
                                                    my hope in the human
I remember the Christian if in peace he will walk as my
                                                    travelling companion
I remember the Muslim strong at my side as a brother
I welcome the learned and all who can spell me ways and
                                                    methods of doing
I remember John Brown, for his courage and manhood still march
                                                    on in America

Highest above all let me praise Marx Lenin and Stalin
Marx for he taught us our power the strength we enfolded
                                                    together
Stripped bare the false mysteries our enemies clogged in our
                                                    seeing
Lenin who made this truth clean clear as a fountain our common
                                                    possession
Lenin man's best of men touching bright as a summer sun
The heart unspoilt by hate of its fellows
Stalin who labours that in each this truth shall root in its glory

In these and with these I remember the ordinary man in any
                                                    street or village
Who ever held out to me the hand of a brother

I grasp this hand wherever I find it in Perth Paris Prague New
York Buenos Aires Peking
This hand piled flowers in my praise red roses in Prague
All the earth's blooms gathered in Moscow
I hold with particular tenderness the hand of a German woman
Fled from the Nazis because she saw herself demeaned in their
thinking about me
Look this is a white hand it is my hand I am the black man.

I hear strong voices calling me brother from the rough horse-hair
tents of Mongolia
In Korea the rivers and mountains leap with the cry of their
welcome
My heart sings in the lilt of the tear-twisted caress from the
mountains and far lands of China
I gather like greeting from the red roughened hands of the
steelmen of Sheffield
My smile is the smile of the miner descending the coalpits of
Rhondda
I am by the side of the stevedore heaving bales in the
shipyards of Antwerp
I reach around earth to embrace the Australian docker
For his handclasp assures me victory over subtly plotted
deception

These are my strength my force their varied conceivings
My calm that in them my living may never decay

And since I am of Africa all that is Africa comes with me
Striding hot storm we come tenting our courage and hope
With the hope and the courage of the men of America Europe
Australia and all the sea islands
The good men the true men the strong men the working men
Whose sweat is their daily bread whose strength is their class

Scientists craftsmen teachers painters poets philosophers come
We shall work till our power invested together create a new
world

Till there be no longer famine in India
Till the Yangtse flood no more
Till we plant gardens in Gobi
Till we gather each year the harvest of the Sahara
Till our force bright as the atom blasts the evil oppression which
cripples all our creations

And so, I rest the little blond German child gently against me
I trace the years with him
I rest the little black African child gently against me
He and the German boy trace the years with me
I rest the little Kamchatchuan child gently against me
I rest the little Georgian child gently against me
She and the little Japanese boy trace the years with me
Let our love hold them till bright as the atom together
Their power blasts the evil oppression which cripples all our
creation
Till man cover the earth with his glory as the waters cover the
sea.

Joseph

Come walk with me
And hear a tale of a woman
Grounded thus
That spite all seeming
Man is still Earth's first wonder

This tale is of a woman
A woman taken in adultery
Somewhere, anywhere
In a modern town
In the United States of America

She was a young woman
A white woman
For there are white women
And black women and red women and brown women
In the United States of America

I will show her as I knew her then
Body parts and passions
Speaking fit for love
Nothing of too little or too much
All in a just proportion

Thighs firm round
As breast and leg
A skin of ivory whiteness
That companioned hair which fell
The riot of a sunset
Caught midst copper beeches
A spirit bright and gay
All movement

Hers was a way
Unflecked by wantonness
Yet though no wanton
She was taken straight
In the act, the very act
Like her of bible story

Snared in the mesh
Of love's need circumscripted
Sore thrust down-daunted
Of no other gage
Save male or female
Sorted in their kind

This woman's name by marriage I withhold
Though of course she had a name in marriage
All men and women have such names
In the United States of America
Black men and women all excepted
South in these States
Plain John or Mary these
Rastus sometimes, sometimes simply Sam
It would not do to credit dignity
To dogs or negroes there

Her husband was a lawyer
Busied with cares and tastes
Which spared him thought of little
Could entwine his duty laid
At bed or beard with her his whole being fled
The riotous entail of pleasure his wife's young lips
Conjured from out her longing
Scarce lintelled in her womanhood
He thrust her from him
At twenty she was left alone in all her beauty

Some in this case are known to cry their need aloud
Some scrabble anguished
Rough ashes from the past, dry-mouthed
Of hopes long dead
And passions ruminate
Her shame she hid from every eye but one

There was a man who served about the house
A black man by the name of Joseph
His were the rough tasks of the household
He cleaned the furnace exercised the dog
Drove cars filled other lowly chores
Black men and women sometimes find to do
South in these States
The United States of America

Gentle and quick to please
Polite to hear a tale
However oft repeated of another's sorrow
He knew and kept his master's secrets
Shared those of his mistress too
Constrained in strife
To strip two aching hearts the debt they could not pay
Of happiness
Love's clients snared consuming bitterness

Now Joseph was a young and bonny gaillard
Tall slim and lissom
As a fir tree sprung
Not unfamiliar in the ways
Of stately matrons of the upper classes
Who one while sedate demure face cast down
Will private bridle nought their reins up toss them
Grounded in birdlime once this trap had galled him
And though not like his namesake timid in advancing
He was thereafter discreet in this guise

Swift treacheries he knew stalked a too-willing faith
Save where this faith adhered a rarer bail
Then sudden passions taught
Nor was he anyway disposed
To pay the price some pleasures sometimes carried
For men like him
In the United States of America

So when his mistress spoke her sorrow to him
He listened kindly as ever was his wont
And shaped his way
As fitted one who trod the dangerous day
Of close familiar to a young wife left
Alone in all her beauty

Yet well 'tis known
Men may not live alone
Nor women neither
Ask these young virgins here
What they would choose complete
The life that flames within them
Or these censorious old maids
Bid them tell how stem
The hell that rages in them

Stop here's a parson
Let him prose awhile
How he came bare his need
To some shrewd spavined whore
Who teased his bondage sore
In slow decline or unappeased consent
Till husband she made life clamourous and rude
Or take a bishop
Strictest and straightest of this set
August austere aloof he stands
Wrists bound about with crimson bands

Scarlet for blood and sin
His thin-lipped visage sour as the wine
Christ's blistered lips refused on Golgotha
Any choir boy knows what ails him

And so these two alone about the house
Still canvassed matters
Men and women find for comfort in all tongues
Till Joseph far the wiser of the two
Took to pondering with himself how this would end
For he was no Adonis and he had eyes to see
His mistress radiant again
How simply now she shared her thoughts
Of simple things with his
Would ask him how an ornament became her
Or how a curl this way or that disposed
Called out her beauty
Whether a dress well mated with her hat
Would make her sure of pleasing
When she visited in town
How never now for good or ill
She made mention of her husband

Subtly in the interplay of life's small fictions
He divined her mood knew her at length
Absolved the thoughts her wealth and station
Had till now confined her
Strong flesh engrosses love
Love edges indiscretion
So at last with great regret
He thought it best to find some other service

She for her part was not much moved at first
For servants cost but little
The next day brought a handy man
As useful as was Joseph
But soon she found
The house all empty as her life
In her experience never thus before
An emptiness that harboured all about her
A something had gone out
That told life's smallest actions to some purpose
And gave them savour
But this could not be Joseph
He had been a servant nothing more
Willing 'tis true accepting tasks
As something he had pledged himself to do
And therefore must do well
So was this other and as sober
And yet….. the thought first raked her blushing
It could not be that from a servant she had hoped
More than the work she paid him
This monstrous thought she fled
To wildness of gay living
Astonished all who knew her
But often in the midst of some bright chatter
She would start absent and silent leave her friends
Brooding some hope that sudden warmed her blood
Until at length forthright and plain
Knew 'twas his smile had warmed her blood
That he had lit dark corners with his laughter
Know him alone of all men mirror to herself
And forthright as her temper sought him out
And wrote him all her mind

'Why did you leave me when you knew
All that I have was always yours for asking
I speak not of possessions for those still are
As always you must know they were
Yours for the taking
But what I am
When I stand naked to myself
I am for you alone
Body mind nor passion
Shall share with any other
If I may not with you
I may not now in any wise command you
Nor did I ever for well you know
When you were with me how we stood together
But if you do not hate me come at least this once
And let me see you
For house and life alike are empty now without you
And if you will not come as I would have you come
Come for past friendship
But come once more and let us speak together.'

This note she sent by messenger to Joseph
For patient searching had found out where he lived
With a Senator in the town
In it she also gave him rendezvous
A point some four miles out of town
Where on a mound o'er topping the pine woods
Which skirt the outward suburbs
There was a grassy hollow hidden from all eyes
Above or down
Where the whole country round about was clear
A favourite spot of hers in adolescent days
When in the strange new thoughts which thronged her mind
She had longed to be alone with time
Here now her fancy told her to bring Joseph
In latest age she would recall
This first and last tryst that they kept together

How fresh from her bath she dressed
All in clean linen
Combed her hair straitly
And with shy sweetness touched
Each firm round breast and lip
For she would be her best ambassadress in love
Nor knows she yet how as they stood conversing
Scarcely met
Wild ruin came to thrust them separate forever

For Joseph had been careless
Had put by her note
Where he shared lodging with another servant
Who meanly read it and Joseph once gone out
Opened its message to the Senator their master
Now this old man had been
Of those who sought to glean
Where the woman's husband had neglected
And forthwith followed Joseph
Hot with intent to trap them
And to assure his safety and for witness
Brought another with himself
Leaving word that more should trail them
So these two aged lechers ran
Short pulsed and gasping
Malice edging their thin rages
And as they ran still figured all her parts
From knee to navel
Limb and clothing tumbling one disorder
Soft tissue ruffled rose to rose
Her volleyed loins deep slopes of hot destruction
Thwart which desire swept them toppling on her breast
Her whole form spent in pleasure
A Leida in her dalliance
Her hair the great betrayer framing her flushed face
A Leida who for swan-time had chosen a black swan
All this and more they pictured came near and stood amazed

What she there said to Joseph
Silence must always hold
What 'er it was he touched past tears
Clasped her close to him his hand on her bowed head
While she sobbed out her woe upon his shoulders
Till from the ways where sorrow dries the tongue
Her weeping ended she raised her head
And shyly smiled upon him
So these two old men found them
Amazement held them speechless but not long
For here was worse far worse than they expected
A woman seized constrained in short a rape
They had almost hoped
It was well known all black men lived
With this one thought in mind
But to find him thus consoling her
With quiet understanding calming her
Oh! What a smile there was upon her face
This was too much
God damn the nigger!
This was pretending that he was a man
Rape called for death
This called for sudden death
They whistled up the posse to ensure their man
And Joseph and his friend then only sensing mischief
Saw them and bade Joseph go and quickly
For well she knew the customs of this South
Of God's own country
And Joseph, nimble feet as any greyhound
Vanished from their sight as from this story

You will remember her of bible story
You will remember how her husband found her
And how in anguished jealousy he sped
His peers to sit in judgement on her
How they in turn to prove him culpable
Led her to Jesus who some said loved sin
And how he stooped and wrote upon the ground
The while the elders waited for some word of censure
How at the last he raised his head
To question at what point with them
Like need had stripped their gleanings of all caution
How at this the old men left him
You will remember how tearless she taken stood
Waiting her condemnation
Strained in anger
At the purposive frustration of her debt
Her form all whipped by pain of mingled shame
Her heartbeats shocked with fear
Raced in wild music
How Jesus bade her go
'for I do not condemn thee'
How at this word her tears did bathe his foot
That he so tenderly should touch her
So gently brush in intimate compassion
The veil that hung her need

So stood this matron while alone with her
The old men leered their gall-dried lust upon her
Her fear was not for self
'twas all for Joseph
Till they mistaking this
Began to make lewd bargains for their silence
When sudden in a rage she drove them furious from her

Jealousy is a carping thing
Nor need it claim possession
Now back to town these aged lechers run
Crying high scandal
Here was no Jesus but they had the sheriff
Burst in upon him and with eager name and gesture
Told all their late adventure fairly glossed
With circumstantial detail of their making
'We found her sprawled the bitch
In the heat of the afternoon
Each nerve surrendered to a black man
Hard upon her'
The sheriff asked not where, what, when
He seized his gun cried
'Where is the nigger?'
But the crowd philosophers in this kind
Wisely had forestalled him
It was not Joseph
He had long distanced harm
But it was another anyone would do
A man had touched forbidden fruit
'twas what they said
A man must die God has so ordered
When he set death the fee of knowledge
To Adam out of Eden

Each worship has its rites
Now these rawboned rumbustious ignorant men
Worshipped the phallus
Standing stiffly conscienceless
On guard over race-purity
No one guarded women's purity or man's
Incest, syphilis lice gonorrhoea bastardy
Took care of this in whore-houses
And pox-marked adultery
But for a breach of race-purity
The crowd needed a living symbol

To offer to their faith
A black man any black man
Young or old would do

Such are the great occasions
The graver moments when
In high exalting passion
Young and old together
Rich and poor
Riot in worship
Babes in arms
Held high to see
What matrons in a holiday mood
May touch nor blench their anguish
Black phallus stuffed with blood
Acrid as the incense
Burnt of the holy cross
Shredded now for relic
To preserve the race
Created out of Eden man
To only man

So the dervishes danced with the infants
And these held Venus wide for Mars
And some sang high
And some sang low
Till in a still small voice he cried
Then died

Here ends my tale
But some have questioned what men did in this town
While hanging was afoot
The little I have learnt I here set down

What did the liberals say?
The liberals were busy indicting the rights of democracy
In Hungary, Italy, Rumania, Ecuador, Chile, Peru
Outer and Inner Mongolia, anywhere outside the United
States of America
Some called on their congress from the forty-eight
States assembled to urge on their government the need
To ensure the life and liberty of Archbishop Minzenty
Some pressed love's charted freedom as the mainstay
Of Society, urging that this was freedom inalienable from
the pursuit of happiness
For that love sexual, homosexual, heterosexual, bisexual
any set

you will was the citizen's right whenever need sat upon him.
Some to prove it came with their neighbours' wives,
Some with their neighbours' sons and when the
Alarm sounded were somewhat delayed while they
took their hands from their neighbours' bosoms and
other parts privy to passion
But when it was rumoured that this freedom
was being exercised by Negroes they passed a
resolution denouncing communism and in their
persons forthwith rushed out to suppress it
What did the parsons say?
Some stood on the edge of the crowd and gave their
blessing, Some argued God's law who had given the
Negro as a brother with this most agreed saying
'We own God's law is good we do indeed take the Negro
as our brother
But still we have a better that never shall we own a Negro
In our sister's bed a brother-in-the-law'
What did the workers say?
The workers said nothing
What did the workers do?
The workers did little
Many were in the crowd, most stayed indoors some
wrote to the newspapers some held meetings and
advised the Negroes not to provoke their fellow
citizens to violence

But some there were who plainly denounced the acts of the mob
Who plainly said that men must be found equal
Not only in the words of the Fourteenth Amendment
But as they walked the streets of the towns where they
                                    lived together
In the factories and fields where they worked together
In the schools where they learnt and played together
In the choice of their mates and in the books which they
                                    read together
They further shewed that men must be resolute if they
                                    would find equality
To remove whatever might stand in the way
Not least the men who plotting to destroy all equality
Set black against white Pole against Irish
Russian against Jew and Jew against Christian
And in a thousand ways made men destroy themselves for
                                    their profit
They showed further that no man would be free till this
                                    was in the doing
For that it was Negro in America Today
Korean next day in Asia
Cuban soon after thereafter Frenchman in Europe
While this nastiness went unchecked
Now men of this mind were few
And not greatly privileged
In the United States of America
And often for the mere thinking these thoughts
Were imprisoned beaten and deprived of their rights
But still they continue and though death thin their ranks
The ranks are renewed and continue the battle
That men may be free
And for these what began as a story of violence
Shall end a salute to America
The land of Walt Whitman
Those States remade for man's image one day
A home for the free.

THESE THINGS OF COURSE COULD NOT HAPPEN IN
ENGLAND.

In Memory of Claudia Jones

She said
I walk with the humble
Yet not in humility
We scale the winds
My feet shall be
No swifter than their feet
My limbs shall share
No strength that is not theirs
When we move we move mountains

I live that men may walk together
Work together love together
Live possess this earth together
Till this be done
I may not rest
Till murder sleep
I may not rest
While children weep
A hungry shame unwept
I may not rest
Til this be done
No task too bitter
Nor any way too sore
Myself small purchase of sure victory

Speak to me of death
When I am dead
Then only
Now
I cannot understand
Nor bid death's pride daunt mine

Here room is not spread for tears
Here amid the dust the heart sings
Out of the darkness a voice cries
Light answers light
Leaping from peak to peak.

Art Against Racism and Fascism

Address by Peter Blackman to a meeting organised by Art against Racism and Fascism, at the Garage, Sloane Square, London, 13 April 1980.

What I really want to talk about relates to the name of your organisation, 'Art Against Racism and Fascism'. There I am wholeheartedly with anybody and everybody in the world who takes a stand against the viciousness that is represented by fascism, which is the ultimate conclusion of what we call racism.

I dislike racism because it seems to indicate that somewhere or other there is to be a quarrel about ourselves. For me there are no races, there is only the human race and after that and about that there can be no questioning. The conditions that have produced fascism, of which we have had in our lifetime one of the most brutal manifestations – what the Germans called very glibly 'The Final Solution' – had gone on for a very long time. As I said in my poem, 'My Song is for All Men', *'these things had happened before'*. And in an unpublished part of the poem which has never seen daylight, I say: *'We can still hear the voices of the carrion pack, baying in the instruments of the White Australia Policy.'* These are the sort of things that lead up to fascism.

German fascism, and what it meant in particular, threw us right back on our haunches and made us ashamed, in more ways than one, to be human. It is against that background that I think we should be thinking. If I appear to be moved, I am moved, not by what I have said but by the memories that it brings back. 'My Song is for All Men' came out of actual experience. All my writing is what I call lived experience. There were two incidents leading up to the writing of that poem that particularly moved me. One was a visit to the then unresurrected part of Warsaw which used to be called the Ghetto. I was there on the occasion of a conference, quite by chance, for me. Among the people who were there was a very distinguished English intellectual, Jewish by origin, the late Professor Levy. I remember walking with him through the Ghetto, a grown man of fifty, nearly sixty. He stooped down and he picked up a torah, all bloodied over, and he turned his head away and I had to weep with him. Not because of the torah, but because he had been so hurt. He was a living representative of millions who had gone that way.

And just before that, a much more encouraging thing had happened to me. We were in the days of austerity, there were still rations. I was so poor at that time I couldn't buy a proper suitcase. So a friend lent me one of those clumsy hand trunks, and as I got out of the train at Warsaw, being accustomed to England and little petit-bourgeois pretentions connected therewith, I struggled up towards the platform with this heavy trunk. A strapping boy, gloriously splendid physically, stepped out of the crowd, gripped my bag, took it from the train on to the platform – and I, being acclimatised to petit-bourgeoisdom, started fumbling in my pocket for some change to give him something. He said 'No thank you, I am a Jew.' And it was then I went to the Ghetto in Warsaw that I realised what he meant. I like to think of that boy of 18 now somewhere in the world, still striding forward with his force undiminished, and I hope always on the side of humanity. Because he put me firmly and irrevocably on the side of a lifelong struggle against everything that fascism means, in whatever form it comes.

I remember we all had our quarrels. I belonged then, practically and actively, to the extreme left – but within the extreme left you younger people will remember talking of things like Stalinism and so forth. For us it wasn't Stalinism, it was Stalin, good old Uncle Joe the Liberator and all that. But all honest people, if they were human beings, always had questions and still have questions. I remember saying to a friend, 'Look, I don't agree with everything, as you know. But after what I saw in Warsaw, if Harry Pollitt were to kick me from one end of Oxford Street to the other, I would take it.' For I would have nobody believe that the slightest fissure could be between me and the struggle against the filth that was fascism (Harry Pollitt, for the younger people, was then the Secretary of the Communist Party of Great Britain.)

It is out of that that I, at the age of 70, with not very much behind me, have come along to talk to you about poetry and words. I'm not here to give a special definition of poetry. There is none, that I know, nor of the Poet. We have all had years and years of all sorts of discussions and descriptions, I'm sure, 'the unacknowledged legislators of mankind' and that sort of thing. I don't regard myself as any legislator, unacknowledged or otherwise, and I'm not going to talk about how I write poetry or how I think poetry should be written. If you want to know about poetry, the best thing to do is to read it. One of your earliest and best-known poets of the early nineteenth century described poetry as 'emotion recollected in tranquillity'. But I'm not here with any view about poetry, it is that poetry is 'speech heightened'. That is the only definition I have tried to give to poetry: 'speech heightened'. Of course, speech is concerned with words. You must love words if you are going to be interested in poetry. Above all forms of expression you must *love* words, because I think words are beautiful. Any word, anywhere, all words, in all languages.

Now I think in English, which I call my language. Don't ask me why or how, but it is my language, and if I don't speak it, I would be dumb. If I didn't speak English you might as well take the blood out of my veins, I have no other. To understand that would involve too long a historical excursion. So I would say that one begins by being drenched in words, and although perhaps I have not quite dried out, I was drenched in some of the most beautiful English words from childhood. I was brought up a Christian and spent most of my time up to the age of thirty somehow occupied in reading that very strange book, *The Bible*. Very strange, because it's such a mixture of violence and beauty, and hatred and love. But there it is, it's a glorious book and I think people who are tending to reject its beauty, especially in the form of the King James version, are taking it from the heritage of their children. If you do that, you're not only depriving them of a central part of their intellectual, cultural and emotional heritage – whether you believe it or not or want them to believe it or not – but you're also depriving them of one of the greatest sources of beauty in their experience. I copied out a few verses from one of the most poetic and beautiful books, one of the most beautiful poems in any language that I have ever come across – and that is the Book of Job. I think that the beauty in this case is largely due to the English version, I don't know the Hebrew. God is upbraiding Job for his temporary lack of faith.

> *Where wast thou when I lay the foundations of*
> *the Earth?*
> *Declare, if thou hast understanding.*
> *Who hath laid the measures thereof if thou knowest?*
> *Or who hath stretched the line upon it?*
> *Whereupon are the foundations thereof fastened?*
> *Or who hath laid the cornerstone thereof?*
> *When the morning stars sang together, and all the*
> *sons of God shouted for joy?*

I don't know anything in my experience that can move me as much as that last verse: 'When the morning stars sang together, and all the sons of God shouted for Joy?' And it was absolutely nothing to do with believing in the story of the Creation as set down in the Book of Genesis. It's just the sheer glory and wonder of the expression. That's a good deal more than 'emotion recollected in tranquillity'. It takes you up, God knows where, but when you come back you're never the same person. Now that's poetry.

In a quieter way you might have something very carefully thought, very wondrously fashioned out of a vast experience and a vast knowledge, as was Milton's:

> *Now came still Evening on, and Twilight gray*
> *Had in her sober Liverie all things clad;*
> *Silence accompanied, for Beast and Bird,*
> *They to their grassie Couch, these to their Nests*
> *Were slunk, all but the wakeful Nightingale;*
> *She all night long her amorous descant sung;*
> *Silence was pleas'd; now glow'd the Firmament*
> *With living Saphirs; Hesperus that led*
> *The starrie Host, rode brightest, till the Moon*
> *Rising in clouded Majestie, at length*
> *Apparent Queen unvail'd her peerless light,*
> *And o'er the dark her Silver Mantle threw.*

You'll probably remember that description of early evening from *Paradise Lost*. For me, the pleasure of those lines is just the listening to them or the reading of them. One doesn't necessarily have to understand them, although one grows to understand them. Have you ever understood 'Tiger, tiger burning bright, In the silence of the night'? How many times have you read it? I have read it hundreds, if not thousands of times. I read it before I came here. I still don't understand it. But the glory of it is still there: 'Did he who make the lamb make thee?'

Blake is a glorious poet. But somebody would say, 'but who are you to be claiming to read Blake?' I told you I was an English speaker, but then of course, there is more in a language than the sounds of it. These practitioners, if I may use such a rough word, people like Milton, Shakespeare, Blake, used the language because they loved it and they spoke out of it. They wove beauty out of their own lived experience. It is not an easy thing, even to write two or three collected sentences that will raise your own spirits, let alone somebody else's. It's hard work in the sense of work, you don't just sit down and do it. The word 'poet' comes from the Greek word for 'the doer', it has to be done. Like everything else, you learn finesse and beauty in the doing.

My lived experience was not Shakespeare's. My lived experience was not Blake's. My lived experience was not Milton's, although in many ways, and because I reject difference in races and accept one human race – then Milton in particular and Blake on another scale, do somehow touch my boundaries. In the context of British freedom they fought for what they thought was best. In the context of British freedom for black people, I touch with them. In the context of black freedom I touch with Blake and Milton. There are other people too, of course. There is our good friend, so much rejected in England: Whitman. I think that Whitman has never even been understood in England, let alone much read. But I think he set down a curriculum, a schema. I'm using some ugly words, aren't I? Words more connected with the jargon of Economics. But what Whitman did was to say. 'Look here! Follow this out.' And not many people have taken him out in the English-speaking countries. These few stanzas from Whitman will show you that, apart from the blazing glory of Job or that indescribable delicacy of language in 'Tiger, tiger' which so defeats our rational search for meaning, beauty can come in simple statements:

> *I believe in you my soul, the other I am must*
> *not abuse itself to you,*
> *And must not be abased to the other.*
> *Loafe with me on the grass, loose the stop from your*
> *throat,*
> *Not words, not music or rhyme I want, not custom or*
> *lecture, not even the best.*
> *Only the lull I like, the hum of your valved voice.*

The little one sleeps in its cradle,
I lift the gauze and look a long time, and silently
brush away flies with my hand.
The youngster and the red-faced girl turn aside up
the bushy hill,
I peeringly view them from the top.

or

The runaway slave came to my house and
stopt outside.
I heard his motions crackling the twigs of the
woodpile,
Through the swung half-door of the kitchen I saw
him limpsy and weak,
And went where he sat on a log and led him in
and assured him,
And brought water and fill'd a tub for his sweated
body and bruis'd feet,
And gave him a room that enter'd from my own,
and gave him some coarse, clean clothes,
And remember perfectly well his revolving eyes and
his awkwardness,
And remember putting plaster on the galls of his
neck and ankles,
He staid with me a week before he was recuperated
and pass'd north,
I had him sit next me at table, my fire-lock lean'd in
the corner.

I don't know whether you think that is poetry, but I think it is. And not merely because a man who called himself a poet wrote it. I think it is poetry because of the way in which the man searched for beauty, beauty in the ordinary. That, I think, was Whitman's search, 'beauty in the ordinary'. It is this that engages me most. I have a feeling, and I have thought about this a lot over many,

many years, that we do not appreciate the ordinary enough. That sounds a very banal statement, but we who have claimed to be fighting for the ordinary – left-wing people, to put a label on it, although I detest labels. Our claim is the ordinary, and then so much, and not always at the greatest heights, we're involved in posturing, becoming 'names' and important people, eminences. This is why in so many ways the left disappoints people who cling to it; and from time to time because of this deception and disappointment, they go away resentfully, sometimes in passionate resentment, turn a somersault and become fascists. This search for special treatment, for being exceptional, is something that filters down through the activity of all of us. And in the long run, that is what, and only what, fascism is about: the fight to be exceptional – the master race. They weren't satisfied by being *uber alles*. They had to be the master race, and finally that is just rubbish, there is no master race.

We do not pay enough attention to our exploration of the ordinary. You are ordinary, I am ordinary – I know I am very ordinary. Within a few years I shall be even less than ordinary. So what do we fuss about? Yet it is as such stuff as we that human society is made. What we must try and do is get at the ordinary, and so work that without any suspicion of deterioration we see in the ordinary and *out* of the ordinary that we bring excellence, without elitism. That is what we want – in the ordinary is the excellent. The ordinary people, the ordinary, the men and women who go to work every day. It doesn't matter what they do, out of them comes excellence – not can come but comes excellence. But as soon as we begin to introduce elitism we destroy not only excellence, we destroy the ordinary out of which comes excellence. So particularly to the younger people I would suggest, start thinking, keep on thinking, think always of the ordinary. Don't be put off by other people, think for yourselves. If you're interested in poetry remember that you're occupied with words; you must drench yourself in words, and you must take ordinary words and out of ordinary words you make beauty, you make glory, you make the song of the sons of God when the morning stars first broke out!

Long ago, people thought the same thing. I'll read you these few words by Whitman. He is talking about America, and he says:

> America demands a poetry that is bold, modern and all-surrounding and cosmical as she is herself. It must in no respect ignore Science or the modern, but inspire itself with science and the modern. It must bend its vision more towards the future than the past. Like America, it must extricate itself even from the greatest of models of the past, and while courteous to them, must have entire faith in itself and the products of its own democratic spirit only. Like her, it must place in the van, and hold up at all hazards, the banner of the divine pride of man in himself, the radical foundation of the new religion. Long enough have the people been listening to poems in which common humanity, deferential, bends low, humiliated, acknowledging superiors. But America listens to no such poems.

In whatever words he puts it, I think that is, more or less, with a vast extension, my stand. But before I stop, I should like to read one poem of my own. I take particular pleasure in reading this because some of my contemporaries here would have thrilled with the glory of the action that led to this particular poem. More than for anybody else, I shall read it especially for Alan Bush.

Nobody over sixty can have ever forgotten the thrill of Stalingrad, the agony and the glory of Stalingrad, and the agony of waiting and then the glory of even being alive at the victory! 'Stalin' is now a dirty word, but that does not invalidate Stalingrad, and what Stalingrad stood and stands for; 'Man's unconquerable mind', if I may borrow a phrase from Wordsworth in his sonnet to Toussaint L'ouverture, 'Man's unconquerable mind' – which I am sure will fight even the evils that Stalin induced into the society that produced Stalingrad, and which will go on to victories that will make it impossible that ever again any man – Jew, African, Asiatic, anywhere, should stoop to the dust and weep his shame that those who bore his form should behave in the way the Nazis did. And that is why I came along today.

I am not interested in who reads my poems, who has ever heard of me. I am for the most part concerned really with trying to be alone, but anything that has anything to do with this – it is not an easy task, it requires great thought. The older people will tell the younger, 'it has been tried, it is always being tried, it is still being tried, it is not easy.' But don't get disturbed by things like St. Paul's, Bristol or Brixton. Don't get disturbed even by the police. We can beat the police, we can beat all this nastiness! I am confident that we can beat this nastiness world-wide, and in our localities and nationwide in England or elsewhere. But it needs very careful thought, not sloganising, not picking up people's words. And if you'll allow me to stop here, I'll leave the thought to you, keep trying!

Notes

Stalingrad
I first came across this poem in Mary Ashraf (ed) *Political Verse and Song from Britain and Ireland*, published simultaneously by Lawrence and Wishart (London) and Seven Seas Books (Berlin, German Democratic Republic) in 1975. The date of writing is given as 1945, although it may have been written much closer to the surrender of the Nazi armies at Stalingrad in January 1943.

London
This poem as published in the journal *Life and Letters* in November 1948. Blackman lived the greater part of his life in London, near Hampstead Heath (a favoured suburb of the literati) and saw it as his city, a city of poets as well as one of agony, racism and struggle. Yet he loved London and its people, as I found when I went with him to local shops around Belsize Park, where he seemed to know and have friendly relationships with everyone, neighbours and shopkeepers, or in my own Poplar classroom where he very soon established a warm rapport with my students.

My Song is for All Men
Blackman's most celebrated poem was first published in 1952 as a 20 page pamphlet selling for one and sixpence by Lawrence and Wishart in London and New York, and of his poems it is the most reproduced, in part and in whole.

Joseph
Although Blackman gave me a half-typed copy of this poem in 1974, he told me that it had never been published, did not reveal a date of writing and wanted my opinion of it. He describes a virulent British racism in his poem *London*, and the narrative empathy he extends to blacks in the Southern states of the U.S.A. facing the full

fury of Jim Crow racism and struggling for their civil rights probably as he wrote the poem, is powerful and eloquent in *Joseph*, a luminous English narrative poem.

In Memory of Claudia Jones
Blackman read this poem to the Trinidad-born communist militant, New York campaigner, journalist and founder of the Notting Hill Carnival, at her memorial meeting at St. Pancras Town Hall in February 1965. In a recorded message, Paul Robeson spoke of her relentless organising and resistance in New York before she was banished to London in 1955. Two fine books have been written about Claudia. There is Marika Sherwood's *Claudia Jones: A Life in Exile* (Lawrence and Wishart, 1999) and Buzz Johnson's '*I think of My Mother*': *Notes on the Life and Times of Claudia Jones* (Karia Press, 1985) where I first encountered this poem.